I0410925

Date: 03/03/08

VMware ESX Server 3 Configuration Guide

Enterprise Applications Division
of the
Systems and Network Analysis Center (SNAC)

Information Assurance Directorate

National Security Agency
9800 Savage Rd. Suite 6704
Ft. Meade, MD 20755-6704

Warnings

- Do not attempt to implement any of the recommendations in this guide without first testing in a non-operational environment.

- This document is only a guide containing recommended security settings. It is not meant to replace well-structured policy or sound judgment. Furthermore this guide does not address site-specific configuration concerns. Care must be taken when implementing this guide to address local operation and policy concerns.

- The security changes described in this document apply only to VMware ESX Server 3.0.x and VMware VirtualCenter Server 2.x. They may or may not be applicable to other versions of these products.

- Internet addresses referenced in this document were valid as of February 1, 2008.

Trademark Information

TABLE OF CONTENTS

1. Introduction and Background

ESX Server is the core component of VMware's Virtual Infrastructure 3 server virtualization product. Virtual Infrastructure is at the forefront of a rapidly growing server virtualization field. This configuration guide is intended to augment existing documentation by presenting two particular use cases for Virtual Infrastructure and ESX Server, and by discussing specific security and configuration guidance for each.

Virtual Infrastructure 3 is composed of several components: the ESX Server virtualization platform itself, the VirtualCenter Server that enables convenient administration and configuration of ESX Server hosts, and a myriad of additional services provided by these two software packages. These services enable features such as dynamic load balancing, failover and redundancy, and remote virtual machine access. Proper configuration of these components is essential to creating a secure server virtualization environment.

1.1 VMware Configuration Guidance

This document is intended to augment configuration guidance provided by VMware, Inc. VMware support documentation provides step-by-step instructions for performing many of the tasks outlined in this document. Where applicable, references are provided to the VMware documentation.

This document focuses on the differences in configurations for two distinct use cases: server consolidation and remote access. The server consolidation use case represents the "traditional" purpose of server virtualization, that is, running multiple server operating systems within virtual machines on a single platform or cluster of platforms. The advantage gained by virtualization is the sharing of physical resources across the servers. The remote access use case represents a situation where, rather than acting as mere servers, virtual machines are directly accessed by users. Such virtual machines effectively serve as workstations that are used to perform tasks remotely. In this case, the sharing of resources is unimportant. The advantage of using virtual machines is the flexibility that comes with not having to worry about real hardware. It is especially important, however, that remotely accessed VMs be properly isolated from each other, from the ESX Server host, and from any operational network.

1.2 Definitions

1. **Virtual Infrastructure 3 (VI3)** – A set of software components and services that enable the implementation and management of a virtualization datacenter.

2. **Virtual Environment** – Represents an implementation of Virtual Infrastructure components that are used to provide services.

3. **ESX Server** – The core component of the Virtual Infrastructure package. ESX Server provides the operating system that allows virtualization and the abstraction of hardware resources.

4. **ESX Server host** – A physical server running an instance of the ESX Server software.

5. **Cluster** – A collection of ESX Server hosts, managed by similar policies, permissions, and administrators.

6. **VirtualCenter Server** – A management server that allows for administration of ESX Server hosts through defined users, groups, and permissions.

7. **Console Operating System (COS)** – The operating system used by ESX Server hosts to provide administration and management services, also known to as the Service Console.

8. **MKS Access** – An acronym for **M**ouse **K**eyboard **S**creen Access. Represents a connection to a virtual machine using a client that simulates access to the physical mouse, keyboard, and screen of the remote system.

9. **VMware High Availability (HA)** – A Virtual Infrastructure capability supporting automatic failover protection for virtual machines.

10. **VMware Dynamic Resource Scheduling (DRS)** – A Virtual Infrastructure capability supporting automatic allocation of physical resources between virtual machines.

1.3   Organization of this Guide

This document presents configuration guidance for two possible use cases for VMware Virtual Infrastructure 3. We focus on configuration specifics that differ between the use cases; not all configuration topics are discussed. The document is organized based on the setup and configuration of a new datacenter. It contains the following sections:

Section 2: Determine Your Use Case – Defines the server consolidation use case and the remote access use case. Explains the implications of implementing Virtual Infrastructure 3 in each. Attempts to assist the reader in determining which use case more closely applies to their purpose.

Section 3: Installing and Connecting Physical Network Components– Covers hardware configuration focusing on connection of Ethernet and storage networks. Discusses how to place and configure physical network devices so that they may be integrated with Virtual Infrastructure components.

Section 4: Host Software Installation – Discusses settings and options applied during the installation of ESX Server software on host server systems.

Section 5: Console Operating System (COS) – Focuses on security policies and settings applied to the console operating system of each ESX Server host.

Section 6: VirtualCenter Server – Focuses on the installation and configuration of the VirtualCenter Server. Discusses the placement and configuration of the supporting database, account management service, and related Windows services.

Section 7: ESX Environment Configuration – Covers best practices for setting up and using the virtualization environment after all individual components have been installed and configured. Covers server, guest, network, and permission settings pertaining to the virtual environment.

Section 8: Operational Security Recommendations – Recommendations concerning the use and management of a Virtual Infrastructure datacenter.

This guide assumes a basic familiarity with the roles of ESX Server components such as the Console Operating System and the VMkernel. It also assumes a basic understanding of virtualization concepts such as virtual networking.

1.4   Document Conventions

Most of the configuration guidance in this document pertains to all Virtual Infrastructure 3 use cases. Certain aspects of setup and configuration differ for the server consolidation use case and the remote access use case. Discussions for a particular use case are identified with the following headings:

Server Consolidation Implementation

Remote Access Implementation

Even if your primary focus is a traditional server consolidation use case, it may be useful to consider some of the guidance provided in the remote access discussion. Conversely, you may find that certain aspects of the remote access use case may apply to a more traditional implementation.

2. Determine Your Use Case

In this document, we discuss two use cases for VMware ESX Server: server consolidation and remote access. The former represents the traditional purpose of server virtualization, and the latter is characterized by the needs of a specialized audience. These use cases are not mutually exclusive; it is possible to be in a situation where particular elements of each use case are relevant. For example, an ESX Server may host a virtualized web server that a local administrator wishes to access using the MKS functionality provided by VI3. In this situation, the network and virtual environment would be configured according to the server consolidation use case, but provisions must be made to allow remote access by the web server's administrator which is characteristic of the remote access use case.

Prior to installing and configuring Virtual Infrastructure 3, the implementor should determine network requirements, and determine the use case that more closely matches their needs. The following two sections describe elements of the two use cases.

2.1 Server Consolidation

Server virtualization is intended to address the needs of expanding organizations. As information technology demand increases, the amount of resources necessary to support that demand also increases. Organizations often employ additional server hardware and software to meet these expanding needs. These additional computing resources bring added administrative and maintenance overhead.

Server virtualization seeks to increase efficiency and manageability by providing services specifically designed to address the problem. These services include:

1. Reducing the number of physical systems in the datacenter by consolidating servers that do not use all of their computing resources.

2. Improving reliability by abstracting the server operating system from the server hardware. Failure of a physical server should not result in a loss of service—virtual servers may be moved to other server hosts with no service interruption.

3. Improving computing efficiency by allocating busy virtual machines to idle server hosts.

Virtual Infrastructure 3 is intended to provide easy implementation of services and features that allow these goals to be achieved. Many of the default configuration settings and much of the guidance provided by VMware lends itself to the server consolidation use case. As a result, this document is not intended to be a comprehensive configuration and security guide for this use case. Rather, it intends to discuss some of the more critical issues and the implications of making particular configuration and implementation decisions.

2.2 Remote Access

The remote access use case represents the situation where users need to access virtual machines as workstations or terminals. Such virtual machines may contain software that performs a specialized task or provides particular services that must be accessed by a user across a network. The operation of these virtual machines, including their execution and data, must be isolated within a contained environment.

It is not necessary to connect a virtual machine to a network in order to provide remote access. Unlike typical display-sharing protocol implementations, ESX Server allows a user to connect to a guest without a server daemon running inside the guest. An administrator may configure a virtual machine with no network access, or configure networks that are independent of the network used by the remote access client.

Implementing a datacenter with the intent of providing remote access to isolated virtual machines presents challenges that must be addressed by the implementor. These include:

1. Allowing network users to connect to guests using the management interface necessitates the connection of the operational network to the Virtual Infrastructure management network. Secure implementation requires significantly more network and permissions configuration than would otherwise be necessary.

2. Implementing VI3 services such as VMotion and High Availability.

If users that wish to connect to virtual machines provided by ESX Server are located on an operational network, it is necessary to connect the ESX management network to the operational network. Such a connection must always be mediated because of the opportunity for misuse presented by potentially widespread access to ESX Server hosts. This guide outlines configuration guidance that aims to mitigate the risk created when connecting the ESX management network to an operational network.

Remote access discussions throughout this document consider the configurations and options that are necessary or useful to support this use case. These sections consider the limitations of VI3 to operate in this use case and alert the reader to relevant issues.

3. Installing and Connecting Physical Network Components

3.1 Networking in Virtual Infrastructure 3

There are three types of networks that may be associated with an instantiation of ESX Server: a VMkernel network, a management network, and any number of guest networks. The VMkernel network carries traffic that enables Virtual Infrastructure services such as VMotion and software-initiated iSCSI. The management network is used to connect the service console of each ESX Server host to a VirtualCenter Server and to provide access for management and diagnostics. Guest networks provide an interface to connect virtual machines to each other and to outside networks. The VMkernel network, management network, and guest networks are all virtual networks. Virtual machines and other ESX Server entities, such as the VMkernel and the Console OS, are connected to virtual networks via virtual network adapters. These virtual network adapters cannot be connected directly to a physical network—they must first be connected to a virtual switch within an ESX Server host.

A virtual switch may be associated with a physical network adapter that is connected to an external network, effectively connecting the virtual network to the external network. The three virtual network types may be connected to separate virtual switches and network adapters, or they may share a single virtual switch and physical network uplink. This flexibility allows for easy configuration but increases logical complexity and the potential for inadvertently creating unintended network connections. Figure 1 depicts a sample network configuration within an ESX Server host. In the configuration shown, four virtual network adapters connect to three virtual switches, each connected to an external network using separate physical uplinks.

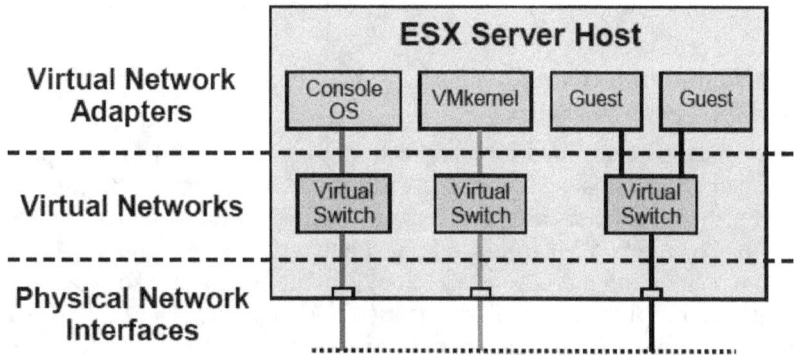

Figure 1. A sample network configuration for an ESX Server host

Creating and connecting virtual networks in ESX Server requires careful planning and implementation. With so many different types of network traffic present in the ESX environment, it is necessary to isolate traffic and prevent inadvertent access to sensitive information.

3.2 Network Planning Guidelines

The physical network configuration of Virtual Infrastructure 3 should be planned during initial setup and installation. Proper configuration of ESX Server hosts and virtual networks can be undermined by an inappropriately configured physical network. In this section we discuss which physical network connections should be provided and how they should be configured.

3.2.1 The management and VMkernel networks should be physically separate.

The VMkernel and management networks should be isolated from each other for security and performance reasons. Each type of network serves a distinct purpose and there is no operational reason to provide access between the two networks.

The VMkernel network might carry both VMotion and iSCSI traffic. Both kinds of traffic are unencrypted. Any system connected to the VMkernel network would be able to observe data stored in the memory of a virtual machine because it is copied between servers during VMotion. Also, the VMkernel network may potentially generate large amounts of traffic—the entire contents of virtual machine RAM are copied over it very rapidly. This may have an adverse and potentially disabling impact on the management network and critical administrative traffic if the two networks are connected.

Ideally, these networks are isolated on separate physical networks. That is, for ESX Servers within a cluster, separate physical adapters and physical switches should be provided for management and VMkernel networks. If switching hardware availability is limited, or physical network adapter availability is limited, it is acceptable to use switching hardware that supports VLANs and isolate the networks using that mechanism. Care should still be exercised in this situation as the demands of the VMkernel network may impact the performance of the management network.

Remote Access Implementation

When configuring a datacenter for the remote access use case if VMotion capability and iSCSI connectivity are not required, a VMkernel network connection does not need to be provided. But if these services are required, the VMkernel and management networks should be isolated onto separate physical networks. If the VMkernel and management networks must be combined onto a single physical network, they must be assigned separate VLAN IDs. The administrator should be mindful of the fact that since user traffic is carried on the management network, the attack surface on the network is greatly increased. If an attacker is able to connect to the VMkernel VLAN, access to unencrypted virtual machine data may be possible.

3.2.2   Guest networks should be physically separate from the VMkernel and management networks.

Guest network traffic destined for a physical network should always be placed on a separate physical adapter from management and VMkernel traffic. It is appropriate to use as many additional physical adapters as are necessary to support guest networks. It may be sufficient to place the management, VMkernel, and guest networks on separate VLANs connected to the same adapter, but connecting them to separate physical networks provides better isolation and more configuration control than is available using VLANs alone. The ESX Server VLAN implementation provides adequate network isolation, but it is possible that traffic could be misdirected due to improper configuration or security vulnerabilities in external networking hardware. It is safer to keep them physically separate.

For example, if an attacker on a guest network were able to gain control of a switch, it would be possible to view and modify all of the VLAN traffic handled by that switch. If the management and VMkernel networks were separated from the attacker by only VLANs, their traffic would be accessible to the attacker, and it might be possible for the attacker to compromise an entire Virtual Infrastructure 3 datacenter. In general, the security implications of physical separation versus separation provided by VLANs should be considered and implemented in an ESX environment with the same care used in a traditional datacenter.

3.2.3   Guest networks should communicate on separate VLANs.

It is generally sufficient to separate guest networks from each other using only VLANs. This is because VMware's VLAN implementation provides adequate security, and there is a greatly reduced threat if a physical switch that carries only guest traffic is compromised.

3.2.4 If it is necessary to connect the VirtualCenter server or management network to an operational network, use an external firewall or a router configured to permit the minimum necessary access.

It may be necessary to provide access to the VirtualCenter server or the management interface of ESX Server hosts from an operational network. But a management network should never be directly connected to an operational network. Such connections should be made only through an external firewall and, if necessary, a network router. If possible, configure the firewall to allow access only from approved IP or MAC addresses. Remote administrative sessions should always be initiated through the VirtualCenter server, so if console access is not absolutely necessary, limit access to only the VirtualCenter server.

Server Consolidation Implementation

In most server consolidation environments, there is no need to access the Virtual Infrastructure management network from an operational network. Access to the management network should be strictly controlled, and if external access is not required, do not provide it.

But if access to the management network and service console of ESX Server hosts is required from an external network, or integration with other administrative networks is necessary, a firewall should be placed between the VirtualCenter management network and the external network. You may consider configuring the firewall with a white list to restrict access to particular external IP or MAC addresses. Also consider implementing a VPN connection inside the firewall or other network device to secure the connection between the VirtualCenter Server and external clients. Connecting to the management network through a VPN provides an additional layer of security when the external network is not trusted.

If access to the console interface of ESX Server hosts is not necessary, but management using the VirtualCenter Server is required, connect the operational network to a separate interface on the VirtualCenter Server. This interface should be configured to use a different subnet than the management network that connects the ESX Server hosts to the VirtualCenter server. This configuration is shown in Figure 2.

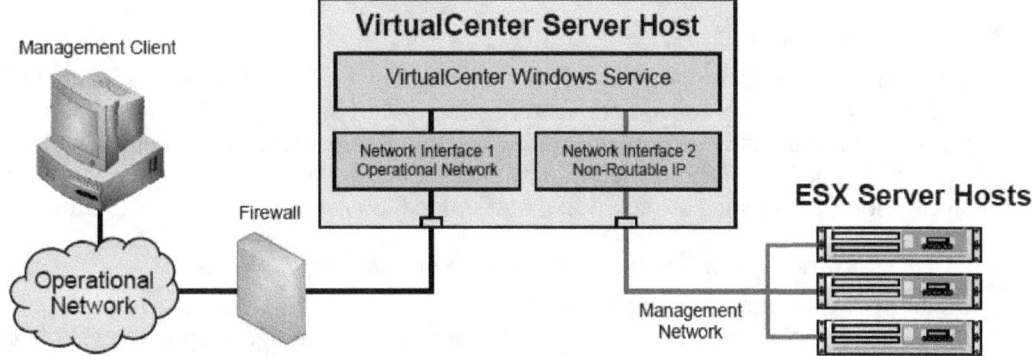

Figure 2. Isolating ESX Server hosts from an operational network using VirtualCenter Server

Remote Access Implementation

Providing remote access to virtual machines presents different security challenges than are presented by the server consolidation use case. Many users of varying privilege levels need to connect to the VirtualCenter server and establish MKS sessions with ESX Servers in order to access guest virtual machines. Such users may not have predictable IP or MAC addresses. If VMotion services are enabled within a cluster, it would not be possible to restrict user access to a particular ESX Server host since virtual machines may move from host to host.

If possible, place users of the ESX Server cluster into a separate VLAN on the operational network. Alternatively, allow users to connect to a gateway VPN which then connects to the ESX management cluster through a firewall. Use of a gateway VPN server allows for detailed connection and session logging, and enables encryption of the console session. Use of a VPN also provides an additional layer of access control.

3.2.5 VLAN trunk links must be connected only to physical switch ports that function as trunk links.

VLANs provide a convenient way to isolate networks when physical network adapters and networking hardware availability is limited. Using VLANs and virtual switches provided by ESX Server, it is possible to create a single virtual network supporting virtual machines belonging to separate VLANs. When a virtual switch that carries VLAN traffic is configured to connect to a physical network uplink, the network uplink becomes a VLAN trunk port.

When connecting a virtual switch to a VLAN trunk port, you must be careful to properly configure both the virtual switch and the physical switch at the uplink port. If the physical switch is not properly configured, frames with the VLAN 802.1q header would be forwarded to a switch not expecting their arrival. This could lead to undesirable behavior, including frames being dropped or misdirected. The Virtual Infrastructure administrator should always ensure that virtual switch uplinks acting as VLAN trunk links are connected only to physical switch ports that function as trunk links.

3.2.6 Physical switch ports connected to virtual trunk ports should always be configured as static trunk links.

Virtual switches do not support topology discovery or dynamic trunking protocols, such as Cisco PVST+. This is because virtual switches have no need to detect connected network devices. A virtual switch cannot connect to another virtual switch or to more than one external physical switch. For this reason, physical switch ports connected to virtual switch trunk ports should always be configured as static trunk links and spanning tree protocols should be disabled. Enabling these services does not provide any benefit to ESX Server and only serves to create unnecessary network traffic and processing overhead.

3.3 SAN Networks

ESX Server supports three types of SAN networking: iSCSI, Fibre-Channel (FC), and NAS. Each type of storage network is suited to different needs. iSCSI and NAS, for example, are more cost-effective than FC and may be implemented using standard network cards, cables, and switches, but may offer less bandwidth and less configuration flexibility. FC is typically more costly to implement, but allows for features such as secure LUN masking and provides superior bandwidth.

3.3.1 Fibre-Channel is the preferred type of storage network.

In an ESX environment, Fibre-Channel offers the added benefit of separating disk traffic from other VMkernel traffic. Fibre-Channel uses a dedicated storage adapter to provide access to storage resources. If a network attacker were to somehow gain access to traffic transmitted across the VMkernel network, storage traffic would not be visible. Also with FC, storage transactions do not compete for bandwidth with other services that use the VMkernel interface, including VMotion. Multipathing may be used to provide redundancy and enhanced performance. (Multipathing setup and configuration using VirtualCenter is described on page 90 of the *SAN Configuration Guide*. [9]) Reference the *SAN Configuration Guide* for additional information concerning the configuration of ESX Server with a Fibre-Channel SAN.

3.3.2 Non-Fibre-Channel SANs should be isolated from other VMkernel traffic as much as is possible.

If iSCSI or NAS is used, it is necessary to connect ESX Server hosts to storage servers using a VMkernel network interface. If possible, create a separate VMkernel interface for storage use only. Connections on all ports not related to storage access should be blocked. The firewall on the VMkernel interface should be configured to allow access on the ports needed for iSCSI or NAS, and a firewall should be placed on the storage server that allows connections only from ESX Servers and other servers relevant to the VI3 datacenter, such as backup devices. Use CHAP authentication to connect to iSCSI servers if it is supported. No unnecessary connections should be made to this network as it can contain large volumes of unencrypted virtual machine disk data.

3.3.3 Mask and zone SAN resources to restrict access.

SAN resources should be masked or zoned to support the principle of least privilege. Only allow ESX Server hosts to access datastores containing virtual machines that they require access to. Do not allow systems other than ESX Server hosts or approved backup servers the ability to access Virtual Machine File System (VMFS) datastores.

Server Consolidation Implementation

VMotion and the services that use it require that both the source and destination ESX Server hosts have access to the datastore containing the virtual machine being migrated. When performing LUN masking or zoning, consider which ESX Server hosts require access to virtual machines and provide appropriate access provisions. VMotion may only occur between ESX Server hosts that have access to similar datastores.

4. Host Software Installation

The ESX Server software is installed onto each physical server that provides virtualization resources. Virtualization resources include processing power, memory, and disk space used by virtual machines. The ESX Server installation procedure is fairly straightforward and uses a graphical installer. This section discusses the settings and options applied during the installation of ESX Server software.

4.1 Connecting Systems to Physical Networks

4.1.1 Do not connect ESX Server hosts to operational networks before they are fully configured.

ESX Servers may be connected to each other during the installation and configuration phase, but should not be connected to an operational network prior to being fully configured and secured. This applies to all physical interfaces on an ESX Server host. This precaution prevents the inadvertent connection of unsecured server hardware to an untrusted network.

4.1.2 Once configured, do not modify connection settings for VMkernel and management networks.

Once software has been installed and configured, the administrator should avoid modifying network connections that carry VMkernel and management traffic. It is easy to inadvertently connect these networks to an operational network, exposing sensitive traffic to the rest of the network.

4.2 ESX Server Host Software Installation

4.2.1 Do not create a default port group during installation.

Creating a default port group during installation may present an opportunity for guests to connect to a management network. ESX Server hosts should never be connected to an operational network during installation. If a default port group is created and left unchecked, an inadvertent connection between the management network and a guest may occur when the server is moved to an operational environment.

4.2.2 Create separate partitions for directories that are likely to become large.

Disk partitioning must be done during the installation of ESX Server software. If installing to a system with an adequately sized local disk, the default partition layout provided by the installer is sufficient. If modifying the partition layout, ensure that separate partitions are created for the /home, /tmp, and /var/log directories. [17,15] Each of these directories could fill up during operation of the server. The administrator should prevent this from happening by periodically reviewing these directories to ensure that space is available and by taking other steps, such as configuring log rotation to ensure they do not become full. If these directories are placed on the root partition and allowed to fill up, the server host may be disabled.

4.2.3 Critical resources should be placed on local storage.

Partitions that support the operation of an ESX Server host or its Console OS should be placed on local disks if possible. If booting ESX Server hosts from a SAN, supporting partitions should be placed on LUN0 of the SAN. Network attached storage cannot be used for the swap space or the core dump partition. [18,8]

The service console operating system swap partition must be at least 544MB. [4,182] The VMkernel core dump partition may not be placed on a software-initiated iSCSI volume. [18,8] Evaluators, VMware technical support, and administrators performing patch testing and deployment may wish to have access to this partition for diagnostic purposes.

5. Console Operating System (COS)

ESX Server software is composed of two core components: the virtualization kernel (VMkernel) and the Console Operating System (COS). The VMkernel manages system resources and enables the core virtualization service. The COS, also called the "service console," supports the operation of the VMkernel by, for example, allowing storage volumes to be mounted and configuration parameters to be set. All user interaction with an ESX Server host, including access via VirtualCenter Server, is mediated by the COS. The COS also provides the local user interface and network services that enable administrators to interact with the system.

5.1 Install only VMware patches and updates on the COS.

The COS is based on a customized version of Red Hat Enterprise Linux. It includes many tools and utilities familiar to Linux administrators, allowing for a simple learning curve and easy operation. But the COS cannot be treated as any other Red Hat Enterprise Linux system. Most of the tools, utilities, and functionality provided by the COS have been modified to explicitly support the specialized ESX file system and network interfaces. For this reason, patches supplied by Red Hat or other vendors should not be installed. Utilities included with the COS should not be replaced. Only patches or updates provided by VMware should be installed.

5.2 Avoid installing third-party software in the COS.

Third party software and services should not be installed in the COS unless absolutely necessary. The COS is not intended to support the operation of additional software or services beyond what is included in the default ESX installation. If the decision to install additional software is made, determine whether a VMware-provided or approved product exists prior to adding an unsupported third-party product. VMware does not support the addition of third party applications that have not been explicitly approved. Always use a test environment to verify that the addition of the third party software doesn't disable existing functionality or security measures.

5.3 Disable or restrict access to unused network services in the COS.

Disable or restrict access to unused network services in the COS. For example, if connections to the web interface of ESX Server hosts are not required, the web server in the console operating system of each ESX Server host should be disabled. Connections to ports for services that are not used should always be blocked using both the built-in firewall and an external firewall.

If all management of ESX Server hosts is performed via the VirtualCenter Server or using SSH, disable or restrict connections to any other service console port. Never allow insecure protocols such as telnet or FTP for service console connections. A list of the default open ports is provided in the *Server Configuration Guide*. [7, 188] Some services and ports provided in the list apply to the VMkernel interface, not the service console interface. Ports that apply to the VMkernel interface are closed in the service console by default.

The *Server Configuration Guide* provides instructions for opening and closing specific ports in the service console. [7, 242]

Remote Access Implementation

Access to port 903 on the service console of ESX Server hosts is required in order to provide MKS access to virtual machines. Ensure that this port remains open and available to outside clients in a remote access situation.

Disabling the web interface of ESX Server hosts does not restrict the abilities of remote access users. Connections to the may be established with the virtual environment using either the web interface or the VI Client provided via the VirtualCenter Server, which provides access control and negotiates the MKS connection with a virtual machine.

In the remote access use case, it is especially important to disable unnecessary services running in the service console. Remote access users have significantly more exposure to the management network than in the server consolidation use case, and there is a much greater opportunity for an attacker to exploit any potential vulnerabilities on the management network.

5.4 Use VirtualCenter for management of virtual machines. Do not use the COS.

It is possible to change virtual machine configuration parameters from the service console shell. In general, reliance on the service console for routine management of virtual machines and performing associated operations is bad practice. An administrator should never implement scripting languages or shell scripts that modify virtual machine configuration because they might interfere with the operation of VirtualCenter services, provide an unmediated mechanism with which to modify configuration parameters, and interfere with the operation of the cluster to which the server host belongs. Additionally, future versions of ESX Server, such as ESX Server 3i, may not include a service console shell, so management practices should not rely on its existence.

5.5 Assurance and Logging

Logging of events and verification of important files is important to ensure that unintentional or unauthorized changes have not been made to an ESX Server host.

5.5.1 ESX Server host clocks should be synchronized using NTP.

ESX Server hosts should have their clocks synchronized for the purpose of keeping coordinated logs for the service console and virtual machines. This is most efficiently done using NTP. The VMware knowledge base article, *Installing and Configuring NTP on VMware ESX Server* [20], provides information regarding configuring ESX Servers to use NTP. The article recommends that servers connect directly to the Internet to retrieve time information, but this practice should be avoided. Instead, provide a separate NTP server for use by ESX Server hosts. Place an NTP client and server on a Linux host with two network interfaces. Synchronize the system clock with an external network using the NTP client, and provide the NTP server service on the internal network. A firewall should be placed between this server and the rest of the management network, restricting access only to the NTP service. A sample configuration is shown in Figure 3.

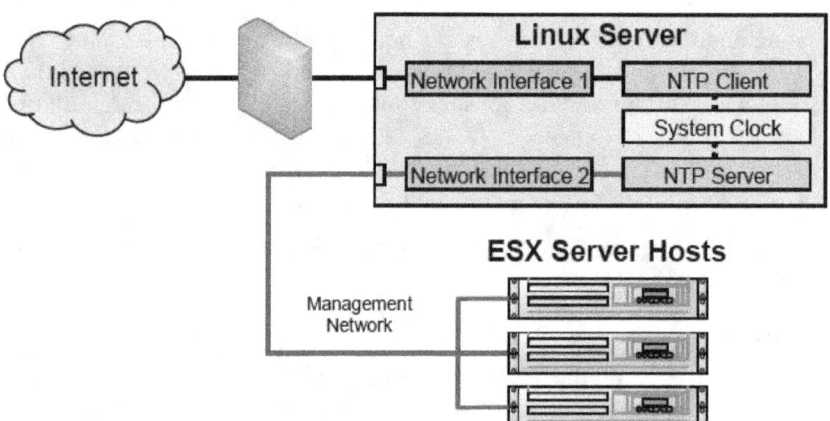

Figure 3. NTP Server Placement and Configuration

5.5.2 Manage log size to avoid filling volumes.

It is important to enable log rotation, cap log file size, and to implement remote logging. Log rotation is essential because log files may grow so large that they fill the volume they are stored on. This must be prevented to maintain logging integrity and prevent a denial of service. An extensive discussion of logging and logging configuration is covered in the *Security Hardening* whitepaper. [17,10]

5.5.3   Implement file system integrity checks and password policies for the COS.

The *Security Hardening* whitepaper covers verification of file system integrity and implementation of password policies. These practices should be followed for every ESX Server host in a datacenter. [17] If password files are going to be integrity checked, it may be desirable to synchronize the password change policy with the file integrity checks to minimize the need to continuously update stored file hashes.

5.6   Account Management and Authentication Configuration

5.6.1   Only server administrators should be allowed to manage the COS.

Access to the service console should be strictly controlled. In either use case, only server administrators should be permitted to connect to and manage the service console. Routine administrative and management tasks do not require access to the service console; these types of tasks should be managed and handled by the VirtualCenter server. Never provide extraneous account access in the service console, grant access only to the minimum number of users necessary.

5.6.2   All root console logins should be disabled.

By default, root access is not available from a remote login, only from the local system console. Root console access to ESX Server hosts should also be disallowed. Create a separate account specifically for local console management and enable su and sudo for the account. After creating the separate management account, disable the ability to login using the root account for both local and remote users. Test the new account before disabling root logins to ensure that you have not been inadvertently locked out of the host system. Detailed instructions concerning limiting root access are provided in the *Security Hardening* whitepaper. [17,6]

5.6.3   Use a directory service such as Active Directory to manage COS user accounts.

If available, use a directory service such as Active Directory for authentication and password management. It is still necessary to create accounts on each server, but their policies and passwords may be managed using a directory service once accounts are created. All users should be managed using the directory server with the exception of the root user and vpxuser, the special user used by the VirtualCenter Server to perform administrative tasks.

If possible, use a directory server separate from the rest of your operational network for management of ESX Server hosts and the VirtualCenter Server. Connecting an existing directory server to the Virtual Infrastructure management network may enable an additional avenue of attack against the server datacenter. [17,6],[19]

5.7   Replace the COS SSL Certificates

SSL certificates stored in the console are used to provide security and encryption for management sessions between the VirtualCenter Server and the COS. The same certificates are also used with clients directly connecting to ESX Servers.

SSL certificates provided in the service console are not signed by a root certificate authority. They are self-signed and are generated at install time using a predefined algorithm that may be vulnerable to attack. If no secure connections are to be made outside of the local management network, the security provided by these default certificates is adequate. Default certificates expire 730 days after installation of the ESX Server host operating system.

If connections are going to be negotiated external to the management network, then the VMware certificates should be replaced with certificates signed by a commercial certificate authority or should be signed by the organization's certificate authority. More information concerning replacing SSL certificates is provided in the *Server Configuration Guide* [7,227] and the document *Replacing VirtualCenter Server Certificates* [22].

Remote Access Implementation

Providing valid and secure certificates is particularly important for the remote access use case. The SSL certificates provide the encryption key used to secure the session established between a remote client and the ESX Server host. The default certificate should always be replaced when allowing remote access users to connect to the management network.

These certificates should be replaced with certificates signed by a commercial certificate authority or should be signed by a certificate authority unique to the organization.

6. VirtualCenter Server

VirtualCenter Server provides management and administration services for Virtual Infrastructure 3. A VirtualCenter Server may be placed on a separate physical server or in a virtual machine within the ESX Server cluster that it manages. VirtualCenter Server requires a host system running Windows 2000 Server or later.

An entire ESX Server datacenter is managed using a single VirtualCenter Server. VirtualCenter Server enables centralized virtual machine control, mediates remote MKS connections, provides remote management services that enable web-based and client-based administration, provides user access and permissions controls, and provides support for features including the Distributed Resource Scheduler (DRS) and VMware High Availability (HA). The DRS, HA, and supporting VMotion services are not available in an ESX Server environment that does not have a VirtualCenter Server. VirtualCenter should always be used when implementing the remote access use case.

6.1 Hosting VirtualCenter Server

It is acceptable to run VirtualCenter Server on its own physical host, as shown in Figure 4, or in a virtual machine hosted by an ESX Server, as shown in Figure 5. Placing the VirtualCenter Server inside a virtual machine makes it possible to leverage the availability and load balancing services that are provided by VI3 and apply them to the VirtualCenter Server itself.

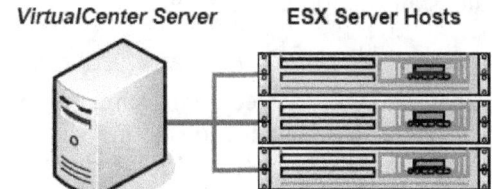

Figure 4. VirtualCenter Server on a separate physical host

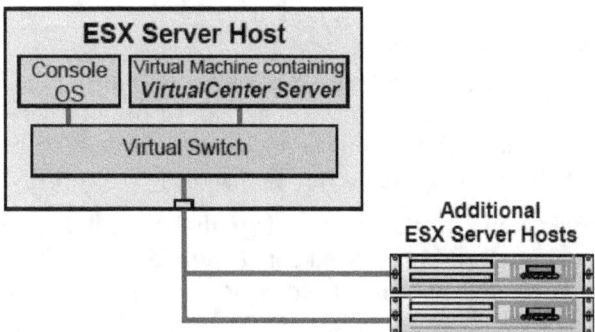

Figure 5. VirtualCenter Server hosted in a virtual machine inside an ESX Server Host

VirtualCenter Server requires a connection to the console network interface on each ESX Server. The guidelines discussed in Section 3.2.1 should be referenced when configuring this connection. The connection details are the same regardless of whether or not VirtualCenter is on a separate physical server or is virtualized within the ESX Server environment.

6.1.1 Connections between VirtualCenter Server and operational networks should be properly mediated.

The VirtualCenter Server should never be directly connected to an operational network or to the Internet without the use of an appropriately configured firewall or router.

Server Consolidation Implementation

VirtualCenter Server should only be connected to an operational network if it is absolutely necessary. If a connection is necessary, determine whether external remote console sessions with virtual machines are also necessary. If not, connect the external network to a separate network interface card in the VirtualCenter Server, and configure this interface to use a different subnet than the interface used to connect to ESX Server hosts. This prevents external users from having unnecessary direct access to the ESX Server hosts.

Remote Access Implementation

In the Remote Access Implementation, users connect to ESX Server hosts through connections mediated by the VirtualCenter Server. This requires the VirtualCenter Server to be connected to an operational network. The operational network should be connected to the management network using the guidance outlined in Section 3.2.4.

6.1.2   *Install the license server on the same host as the VirtualCenter Server.*

The licensing server should be installed on the same system as the VirtualCenter server. The licensing server does not significantly tax the server and placing it on the same host as the VC server ensures that network connectivity or other availability issues do not prevent access to licenses. VirtualCenter handles the licensing for the entire ESX Server environment, and dynamically allocates licenses depending on the current configuration and usage. If the VirtualCenter Server and licensing server become unavailable, ESX Server hosts retain their current licensing permissions and continue to operate.

6.1.3   *Properly restrict access to the VirtualCenter database server.*

The database for VirtualCenter may be located on the same server as the VirtualCenter Server or on a separate system. Restrict database connections to the VirtualCenter Server, a database administrator, or backup software. Do not use the MSDE database included with VirtualCenter in an operational environment. It is not supported by VMware and is not tested to ensure reliable service in a large-scale environment. The *Installation and Upgrade Guide* [4, 57] provides instructions for preparing an Oracle 9*i* or 10*g* database for use with VirtualCenter Server and discusses configuration specifics for both local and remote databases.

6.2   *Windows Host Configuration*

Follow standard security procedures and practices when configuring the Windows Server host that provides the VirtualCenter Server service. Do not create or provide services which are unnecessary— disable unused printing services, file sharing services, etc. VirtualCenter Server provides its own web server that enables web client access, so be sure to disable Microsoft IIS.

The VirtualCenter Server should be kept up to date with the latest Windows patches and available virus definitions, but do not allow unmediated connection to the Internet for their retrieval. Deploy patches using an internal patch management server or via removable media.

6.2.1   *Provide a Static IP address and a host name for VirtualCenter Server*

The VirtualCenter Server should be assigned a static IP address and a host name with valid internal DNS registrations that may be resolved from each ESX Server host. [4, 64]

6.3   *Windows Account Configuration*

Create two administrator accounts for the purposes of installing and configuring the VirtualCenter Server. The default Windows Administrator account should be renamed or disabled following creation of these local accounts. One account is for the initial installation of VirtualCenter Server, and the other is for local configuration and management of the server. The services used by VirtualCenter should be configured to run with the credentials used during the installation of VirtualCenter software.

If a domain controller is to be used for account management on the VirtualCenter Server, the administrator accounts created for local installation and management should not be managed by the domain. In the event of a domain controller failure or related issue, operation of and access to the VirtualCenter server should not be interrupted.

Avoid remote logins to the system using these accounts. Individual accounts should be created for each user that connects to the system remotely. Providing a separate user account for each remote administrator or remote access user allows for proper access control and logging.

6.4 Certificate Considerations

All connections to the VirtualCenter server should use server-certificate verification. The default certificates provided with VirtualCenter Server are not signed by a root certificate authority and should be replaced before server-certificate verification is enabled. [21, 3] After replacing the certificates provided with VirtualCenter, it is necessary to pre-trust the certificate on each Windows client that connects to the VirtualCenter server. The *Replacing VirtualCenter Server Certificates* technical note from VMware provides an extensive discussion of certificate usage and configuration. [21]

Connections to the VirtualCenter Server through the web client use SSL certificates to provide session-level encryption. By default, VirtualCenter Server is configured to allow only SSL-enabled connections from web clients. Unencrypted web connections should not be allowed unless another mechanism is used to provide session level encryption.

Remote Access Implementation

Connections from Virtual Infrastructure clients do not use SSL encryption by default. If remote access users connect to the VirtualCenter Server using the VI client, SSL should be enabled for these sessions. The *Replacing VirtualCenter Server Certificates* technical note provides guidance regarding enabling SSL-encrypted sessions for the VI client.

The MKS session created between an ESX Server host and a client is always encrypted using SSL. If remote access users only have permissions to access to the console interface of virtual machines, it may not be necessary to enable SSL for the management connection, but it is still recommended. The administrator should consider that sensitive information such as login names and passwords may be exposed without the protection provided by encrypting the entire session.

6.4.1 Update VirtualCenter and the Virtual Infrastructure client to the latest available version

Versions of VirtualCenter and their corresponding client software prior to 2.0.1 Patch 1, 1.4.1 Patch 2, and 1.3.1 Patch 2 do not properly handle server-certificate verification during the SSL handshake. Prior to these versions, the X.509 certificate provided to a client at the beginning of the SSL session was not verified. [22] Before deploying VirtualCenter or Virtual Infrastructure clients, ensure that you have updated to the latest available version. Version updates to the VirtualCenter Server software are typically accompanied by updates to the Virtual Infrastructure client. When updating the VirtualCenter Server, updates should also be applied to each client.

7. ESX Environment Configuration

Setting up the virtual environment involves configuring and installing virtual machines, setting policies for administration and management, providing user accounts, setting access permissions, connecting virtual machines to virtual networks, and deploying virtual machines. Configuration of the virtual environment should begin only after physical networking components have been properly installed, ESX Server hosts have been configured, and the VirtualCenter Server has been configured and secured.

7.1 Connect to the Virtual Environment using VirtualCenter, not the COS

VirtualCenter Server acts as a centralized point of entry for configuration and management of an ESX Server datacenter. The virtual environment should always be configured via the VirtualCenter Server unless controls for performing a particular configuration task are only available in the service console. Some tasks may be performed only from the VirtualCenter server including migrating virtual machines between ESX Server hosts and setting up Dynamic Resource Allocation and High Availability services for clusters of servers. VirtualCenter Server provides detailed logging and fine-grained access control allowing for careful control over permissions and the ability to thoroughly audit user actions. This level of control and auditing is not available in the console operating system.

7.2 Virtual Network Configuration Considerations

Association of the service console network interface, the VMkernel interface, and virtual machine network adapters with virtual networks and the physical world may be accomplished using VirtualCenter Server. This section provides general guidance concerning the configuration of virtual networks, and attempts to explain some of the nuances of virtual networking.

7.2.1 Isolate Virtual Machines using Port Groups configured with unique VLAN IDs.

Virtual machine traffic may be isolated using port groups. A port group allows the administrator to define different settings concerning network access and security policy for virtual machines connected to a single virtual switch. As many port groups as necessary may be created for a single virtual switch. Virtual network adapters associated with virtual machines may then be configured to connect to these user-defined port groups. The virtual adapters connected using a user-defined port group inherit and abide by the policies defined within the port group.

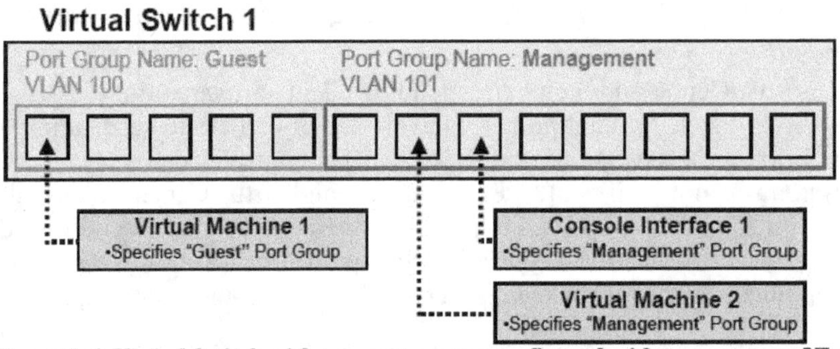

Figure 6. A Virtual Switch with two port groups configured with two separate VLAN IDs

Each port group that is defined within a virtual switch may be assigned a separate VLAN ID. In order to isolate virtual machines using VLANs, create a separate port group for each VLAN and assign it a unique VLAN ID. If two separate port groups within the same virtual switch are created but are assigned the same VLAN ID, traffic is shared between the two groups. A VLAN ID from 1 to 4095 may be specified. Avoid specifying VLAN ID 1, 1001-1024, and 4095. These VLANs correspond to the default VLAN, Cisco-reserved VLANs, and the virtual guest tagging mode. Specifying these modes may cause unexpected operation.

Figure 6 shows three virtual adapters connected to a virtual switch. In order to connect to the virtual switch, the configuration of *Virtual Machine 1* must specify the "Guest" port group. In doing so, its virtual network adapter is connected to Virtual Switch 1 using the policies defined by the specified port group. *Virtual Machine 1* is connected to the switch and placed into VLAN 100. The connections for *Console Interface 1* and *Virtual Machine 2* are similar. They specify the "Management" port group defined on Virtual Switch 1 which connects them to the switch and places them in VLAN 101. In the example, traffic handled by the switch intended for VLAN 100 is visible to *Virtual Machine 1*, but not to *Virtual Machine 2*.

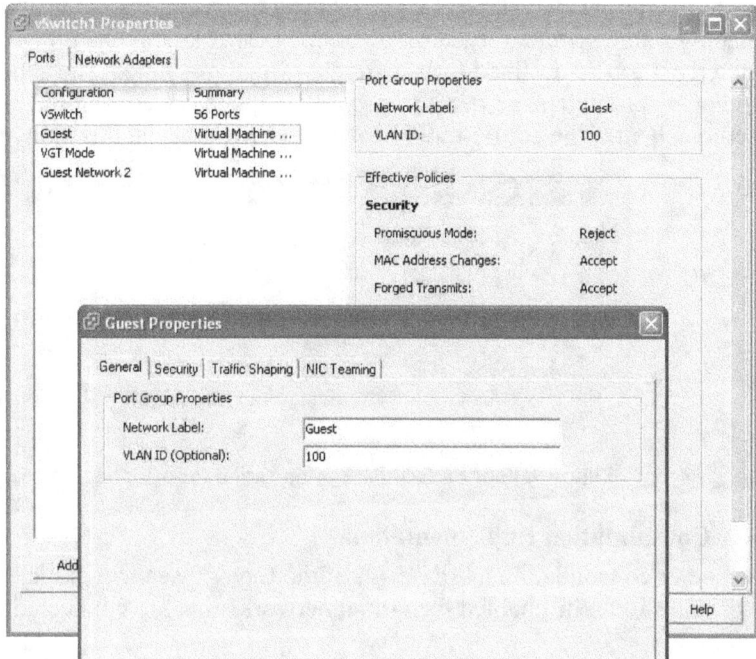

Figure 7. VLAN Configuration using Virtual Infrastructure Client

Figure 7 shows the configuration window for a virtual switch, with the properties window for the port group 'Guest'. In the properties window for the port group, the VLAN ID for the group may be set.

7.2.2 Firewall Configuration Settings and Behavior

Firewall configuration settings apply only to the service console and the VMkernel interface. The firewall configuration settings do not affect the operation of virtual machines connected to a virtual network.

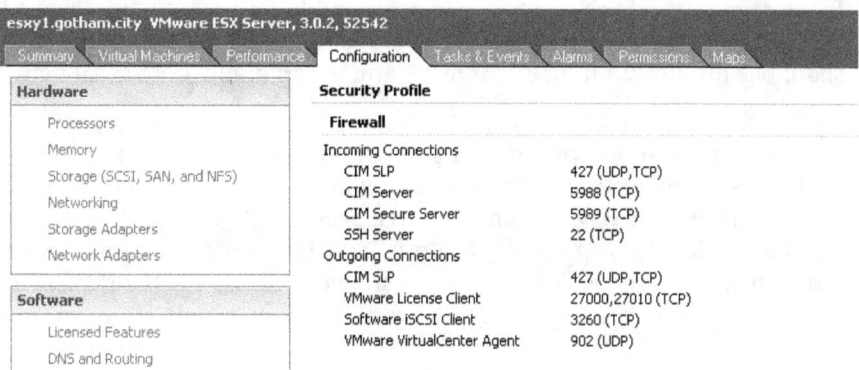

Figure 8. Default firewall settings for the Console Interface on an ESX Server Host as indicated by Virtual Infrastructure Client

By default, the Virtual Infrastructure firewall is set to a 'high' security setting that opens only the ports necessary to perform basic functions and connects to the server using VirtualCenter or the web interface. Figure 8 shows the default firewall configuration as indicated in Virtual Infrastructure Client. Firewall configuration should be further restricted based on operational needs using guidance outlined in Section 5.3 of this document.

7.2.3   Layer 2 Security Policy Configuration

Layer 2 security policies provide enhanced network security for virtual networks. They provide the ability to restrict virtual adapters from entering promiscuous mode and examining all switch traffic, placing frames with a forged MAC on the network, and changing of their own MAC in order to intercept traffic destined for a different virtual machine. These policies may be configured on a per-switch and per-port group level, and are configured using Virtual Infrastructure Client. The configuration pane for a virtual switch is shown in Figure 9.

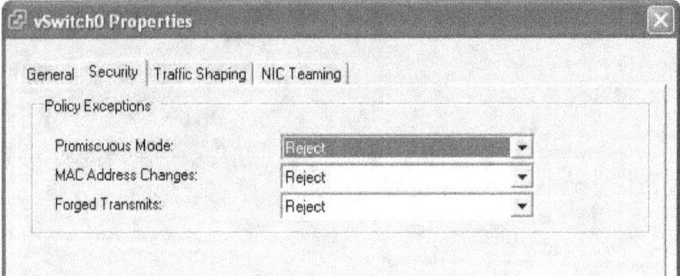

Figure 9. Policy Exception configuration for a Virtual Switch

Server Consolidation Implementation

In the server consolidation use case, all of the Layer 2 security policies provided by virtual networking should be enabled for virtual networks that are connected to an operational network.

In some circumstances, it may be desirable to disable particular security policies in order to effectively implement network security utilities within virtual machines. For example, when implementing an intrusion detection system, it is necessary to allow the IDS to examine all network traffic transmitted on an interface. The 'Promiscuous Mode' Layer 2 security policy would restrict the IDS from being able to examine all network traffic, and must be disabled. In this situation, a special port group should be created and an exception to the policy should be defined, thereby allowing the IDS to examine all network traffic handled by a virtual network.

Remote Access Implementation

In the remote access use case, it may be desirable for users to turn these security policies off for legitimate reasons. If users are permitted to disable or modify the security policies, they should be disallowed from modifying settings pertaining to a virtual network with a physical uplink.

If remote access users wish to configure virtual networks that span multiple ESX Server hosts, these networks should be isolated on their own physical network adapters. A separate virtual network and physical uplink provides much stronger isolation than is available by using multiple VLANs on a single virtual network. This is because ESX Server handles each virtual network as an isolated entity. Testing networks or networks that allow user control over port group or security policies should always be isolated to a separate physical network.

7.3 Virtual Machine Settings

7.3.1 Recommended Guest Configuration Settings

Guest configuration settings provide an additional layer of access control beyond that provided by the standard VirtualCenter permissions controls. This functionality is useful for configuring virtual machines that have been migrated from VMware Workstation to the ESX Server, and placing fixed restrictions on particular virtual machines.

The table below indicates a few of the parameters that may be specified to enhance the isolation of a particular guest. These parameters are set on a per-virtual machine basis.

Configuration Item	Value
isolation.device.connectable.disable	TRUE
isolation.device.edit.disable	TRUE
isolation.tools.commandDone.disable	TRUE
isolation.tools.copy.disable	TRUE
isolation.tools.diskShrink.disable	TRUE
isolation.tools.diskWiper.disable	TRUE
isolation.tools.getCreds.disable	TRUE
isolation.tools.guestCopyPasteVersionSet.disable	TRUE
isolation.tools.guestDnDVersionSet.disable	TRUE
isolation.tools.guestlibGuestInfo.disable	TRUE
isolation.tools.haltReboot.disable	TRUE
isolation.tools.haltRebootStatus.disable	TRUE
isolation.tools.hgfsServerSet.disable	TRUE
isolation.tools.imgCust.disable	TRUE
isolation.tools.log.disable	TRUE
isolation.tools.memSchedFakeSampleStats.disable	TRUE
isolation.tools.paste.disable	TRUE
isolation.tools.runProgramDone.disable	TRUE
isolation.tools.setGUIOptions.enable	FALSE
isolation.tools.setInfo.disable	TRUE
isolation.tools.stateLoggerControl.disable	TRUE
isolation.tools.unifiedLoop.disable	TRUE
isolation.tools.upgraderParameters.disable	TRUE
isolation.tools.vixMessage.disable	TRUE
isolation.tools.vmxCopyPasteVersionGet.disable	TRUE
isolation.tools.vmxDnDVersionGet.disable	TRUE
isolation.tools.guestlibGetInfoDisable.disable	TRUE

Table 1. Recommended configuration settings for Virtual Machines in ESX Server

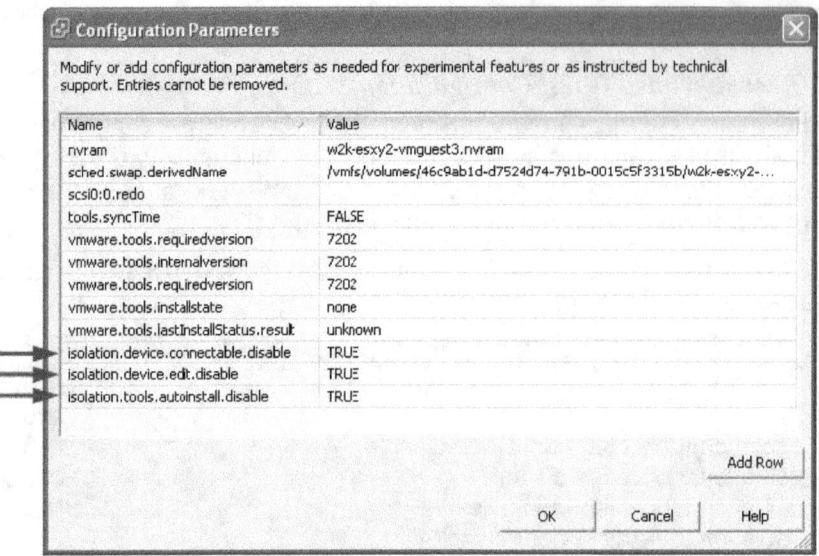

Figure 10. Examples of Advanced Configuration Parameters Added to a Guest Managed by VirtualCenter

7.3.2 Virtual Disk Placement and Configuration

Virtual machine hard disk files and configuration settings are stored in Virtual Machine File System (VMFS) datastores that may be established and configured using VirtualCenter Server. A VMFS datastore may be located on a SAN or the local disk of an ESX Server. The location of a datastore is transparent to the virtual machine. The virtual machine sees the virtual hard disk file contained with a VMFS datastore as a standalone SCSI disk.

Virtual machines may also be configured to have direct access to a logical disk contained within a SAN. The virtual machine can not see any other details of the SAN or scan for other SCSI targets in this mode; it can only see the LUN that has been assigned to it. This mode should be reserved for special circumstances, such as if a special application requires direct access to a LUN. Using virtual disk files is preferred as it allows virtual disks to be easily backed up, copied, and reconfigured. Connecting a virtual machine directly to a LUN may restrict the virtual machine from being migrated using VMotion.

Server Consolidation Implementation

In order for VMotion to function properly, both the source server host and the destination server host must have access to the datastore containing the files associated with the virtual machine being moved.

The use of a SAN provides an additional layer of security control and separation. In addition to the access controls provided by Virtual Infrastructure, access to VMFS datastores may be restricted at the storage level. Configure ESX Server clusters so that they can only access VMFS datastores containing virtual machines that they require access to, do not provide extraneous access. If a SAN used by Virtual Infrastructure contains resources used by other types of server hosts, always restrict access so that VI3 resources are only accessible by ESX Server hosts.

Storage of virtual machine disk files on a SAN allows for simplified and centralized backups. Use of a SAN allows backups to be performed at the volume level. Rather than install backup agents on each ESX Server host and provide open network ports or expensive backup hardware, virtual machine data may be centrally backed up by another device connected to the SAN.

Remote Access Implementation

In the remote access use case, services such as HA, DRS, and VMotion may not be needed. The need for VMotion and backup services must be determined by the system designer. If the objective is to provide a remote workstation or isolation environment, it may be adequate to place virtual machine datastores on disks local to each ESX Server host.

7.3.3   Disable Unneeded Serial Ports and other Virtual Devices

Disable unnecessary or unused virtual devices. Unused virtual devices may allow unintended connections and potentially allow unintended access to datastores. Virtual serial ports, for example, potentially allow access directly to a VMFS datastore. It may be possible to fill up a datastore and inflict a denial of service on a system from within a virtual machine. Unused virtual network adapters may be unintentionally connected to virtual switches, establishing unintended and undesired network connections.

7.4   Permissions and Access Control

VirtualCenter provides the ability to create user accounts and specify permissions with a high level of granularity. This functionality enables administrative tasks to be separated and delegated, and the actions of users to be restricted and logged. Without this functionality, proper implementation of the remote access use case would not be feasible.

7.4.1   Provide Minimal Service Console Access to Remote Users

User accounts, groups, and permissions are defined separately for the VirtualCenter Server and for individual ESX Server hosts. Although some of the default accounts provided in VirtualCenter Server and ESX Server share the same name, they are unique to each system and may have different passwords and privilege levels. Accounts on the VirtualCenter Server and on each ESX Server host are managed independently, and accounts created on the VirtualCenter Server are not propagated to ESX Server hosts.

VirtualCenter Server mediates connections using a special user present on each ESX Server host, *vpxuser*, to connect to and manage ESX Server configurations on behalf of VirtualCenter Server users. This allows users to connect to ESX Server hosts and virtual machines without directly logging into a server host. Do not modify the password or the privileges for *vpxuser*, as doing so may prevent VirtualCenter Server from connecting to and managing ESX Server hosts.

Administrators that do not require console access to ESX Server hosts and all other remote users should only be allowed access to the datacenter by connecting through VirtualCenter Server. In other words, accounts should only be provided on the VirtualCenter Server. ESX Server hosts do not provide the same level of permission control and ease of account management that is available using VirtualCenter Server.

Administrators that require direct access to ESX Server hosts should limit connections to only when absolutely necessary. The majority of day-to-day administrative tasks may be accomplished by connecting through the VirtualCenter Server.

7.4.2   Creating and Configuring User Accounts and Groups on VirtualCenter Server

VirtualCenter makes use of Windows account services to support the management of users and groups. Accounts may be managed on the VirtualCenter Server host system or using an Active Directory server. Users logging into VirtualCenter Server must have a Windows account, although the privilege level granted in Windows does not need to match the privilege level granted for VirtualCenter. For example, a VirtualCenter administrator may be a Windows 'User', but is granted administrative privileges for VirtualCenter.

VirtualCenter Server administrators should not login using Windows administrator accounts. Do not use the Windows *Administrators* group to manage administrative accounts for VirtualCenter.

Create a separate user group for management of VirtualCenter administrators and grant minimum privileges to the group members for the Windows host. VirtualCenter administrators do not require any host administration capabilities or the ability to login to Windows on the VirtualCenter Server system. Do not add the default Windows 'Administrator' account to the newly created VirtualCenter administrators group.

Connections to the VirtualCenter Server should never be made using an account with administrative privileges for the Windows host. Create separate accounts for remote access and grant administrative privileges only within VirtualCenter, not Windows. If the account were to become compromised the amount of access gained by an attacker is limited. This also provides enhanced logging and auditing abilities.

Groups should be created for each type of user that connects to the VirtualCenter Server. For example, 'Datacenter Administrators', 'Virtual Machine Administrators', and 'Limited-Management Remote Access Users' might be three useful groups. Groups are used to grant or deny privileges for some set of objects within VirtualCenter.

If using Active Directory for account management, also provide a local administrative account that allows connection to the VirtualCenter Server in the event of a domain controller failure.

7.4.3   Granting user privileges for VirtualCenter Server

Access control in Virtual Infrastructure 3 is described by three core concepts:

1. **Privileges** – The ability to perform specific actions or read specific properties. All of the privileges available in VirtualCenter are described in Appendix A of the *Basic System Administration [5]* manual.

2. **Roles** – Collections of privileges. Roles are used to aggregate the privileges necessary to perform tasks.

3. **Objects** – Entities upon which actions may be performed. Examples of objects are ESX Server hosts, virtual machines, and even entire datacenters.

Permissions in VirtualCenter are defined by creating a relationship between a role, an object, and a user. VirtualCenter Server includes three 'System Roles': *No Access, Read Only,* and *Administrator*. These roles may not be modified and provide three basic levels of access control. Custom roles may be defined that allow very precise control over what actions a user may perform within VirtualCenter Server.

The VMware *Roles and Permissions Guide* [23] provides a detailed discussion concerning creating users, defining permissions, and enabling user access to VirtualCenter Server. The reader should review this guide during the process of creating users and groups and assigning privileges to those entities. The guide also discusses multiple-privilege conflicts and the effects of propagation in the virtual environment.

Always follow the principle of least privilege when creating custom roles and granting users access to objects. Administrators should have privileges added from the "top down"—grant access to the parent object and remove privileges as necessary. For example, deny administrators the privilege of accessing the console of a guest that is being used for remote access use. Users should have privileges added from the "bottom up"—grant access at the lowest level. If a remote access user requires access to only one virtual machine, allow access to only that particular virtual machine.

8. Operational Security Recommendations

8.1 File System Hash Verification

Create hashes of configuration files in the ESX Server service console and use them to periodically verify that files have not been unknowingly modified. Certain files may change during the course of normal operation, such as files containing password hashes and shadow files. It may be beneficial to align hash verification policies with the password change policy.

8.2 Implement a Structured Password Policy

All components of Virtual Infrastructure should be protected using a strong password policy. VirtualCenter Server has full control over ESX Server hosts, so even if ESX Servers are protected by strong passwords it may be possible to obtain access by exploiting a weak password on the VirtualCenter Server. Follow established organizational guidelines or other published guidelines to establish policies for the length, complexity, and longevity of passwords used for Virtual Infrastructure.

The *Server Configuration Guide* provides an outline of the default password policies used by the Console Operating System. Instructions are provided concerning updating and modifying policies within the COS. [7, 243] VirtualCenter Server passwords are managed by Windows and the usual procedures for setting policies and expirations apply.

8.3 Access to Virtual Machine Templates and ISO Images

When installing software in guests, ISO images should be used in place of physical media connected from client systems. ISO images may be mounted using the Virtual Infrastructure Client by users with the appropriate access privileges. ISO images may be located on VMFS-based and NFS-based volumes. They may not be accessed from the service console.

8.4 Deployment of Virtual Machines

Create baseline virtual machine templates to speed up virtual machine deployment and to establish a reliable baseline configuration. The use of templates minimizes the time required to install operating systems and reduces the amount of removable media that must be introduced into the virtual environment during the provisioning process.

Appendix A: VMware Configuration Resources and References

Appendix A contains a list of VMware configuration guides that are useful for the installation and management of VirtualCenter Server and may be referenced in this document. These documents are available from VMware at: http://www.vmware.com/support/pubs/vi_pubs.html. Documents referenced in the text are preceded by an italicized numeral. All documents listed are published by VMware and pertain to the following products: VMware ESX Server 3.0.1, VMware ESX Server 3.0.2, VirtualCenter 2.0.1, and VirtualCenter 2.0.2.

1. Introduction to VMware Infrastructure, *Revision: 2006-09-25*

2. Configuration Maximums for VMware Infrastructure 3, *Revision: 2006-12-08*

3. Quick Start Guide, *Revision: 2006-09-25*

4. Installation and Upgrade Guide, *Revision: 2006-09-25*

5. Basic System Administration, *Revision: 2006-10-05*

6. Virtual Infrastructure Web Access Administrator's Guide, *Revision: 2006-09-25*

7. Server Configuration Guide, *Revision: 2006-09-25*

8. Resource Management Guide, *Revision: 2006-08-24*

9. SAN Configuration Guide, *Revision: 2006-09-25*

10. Virtual Machine Backup Guide, *Revision: 2006-09-25*

11. Setup for Microsoft Cluster Service, *Revision: 2006-08-18*

12. VirtualCenter Database Sizing Calculator for Microsoft SQL Server, *Revision: 2007-06-01*

13. SAN System Design and Deployment Guide, *Revision: 2007-03*

14. Guest Operating System Installation Guide, *Revision: 2007-11-26*

15. Virtual Machine Mobility Planning Guide, *Revision: 2007-10-18*

16. Patch Management for ESX Server 3, *Revision: 2007-09-06*

17. VMware Infrastructure 3 – Security Hardening, *Revision: 2007-07-16*

18. VMware ESX Server 3 – Best Practices for VMware ESX Server 3, *Revision: 2006-06-05*

19. Enabling Active Directory Authentication with ESX Server;
    http://www.vmware.com/pdf/esx3_esxcfg_auth_tn.pdf

20. Installing and Configuring NTP on VMware ESX Server, *Revision: 2007-04-03*;
    http://kb.vmware.com/kb/1339

21. VMware Infrastructure 3 – Replacing VirtualCenter Server Certificates,
    http://www.vmware.com/pdf/vi_vcserver_certificates.pdf

22. Enabling Server-Certificate Verification for Virtual Infrastructure Clients,
    http://kb.vmware.com/kb/4646606

23. Managing VMware VirtualCenter Roles and Permissions, *Revision: 2007-04-04*